L Yancy

SAVANNAH

Her History

Signed: Louise Yancey Stued

SAVANNAH

Her History

As seen by the artist

Louise Yancey Streed

Narrated by the artist

Published

by

NOSTALGIA, INC.

Guyton, Georgia

1995

LOUISE Y. STREED ©

Dedication

This book is dedicated to my husband, Bill, who has encouraged and inspired me in all of my adventures in art. He is essentially responsible for the publication of this book.

To the memory of my mother and father, Ethel and Elmer Yost, who nurtured my artistic bent from the beginning.

4

SAVANNAH, Her history as seen by the Artist.

ISBN 0-9648581-0-X

Published by: Nostalgia, Inc.
P.O. Box 510
Guyton, GA 31312

Designed by: Douglas M. Eason
Havana, Florida
The artwork produced may be purchased through the Publisher.
The die copy on front of cover is old railroad station.

Acknowledgement

Philip Saraf, fellow artist who often joins me in outdoor on-site painting trips. His insistence that I publish a book motivated me to do just that. It was he who suggested a text in the first person.

Steve Shetsky, artist and art teacher, I appreciate his thoughts and encouragement.

Dr. John Duncan, Professor of History at Armstrong State State College. His encouragement and assistance is selecting historic material was invaluable.

Diane Reardon, who patiently typed and retyped copy and helped in the many, many things it takes to bring a book into being.

George McGuire, publisher and author, appreciated my paintings of Savannah and encouraged me to put them together in this book.

Bill Streed, a renaissance man, was the driving force and facilitator in every way. He engineered us through the process, researched historical facts and planned the logistics.

Olivia Allison, curator of the Owens-Thomas house.

Esther Shaver, her assistance in planning was essential.

Lillie Little of Oglethorpe Marble Company for her assistance in providing information on monuments.

Bob Porter, historian for Solomon's Lodge Number One.

Mrs. I. M. Koger, for graciously allowing me to paint her garden.

Ruth Ramsay for her interest and assistance.

5

SAVANNAH SQUARES

A. Franklin Square
B. Ellis Square
C. Johnson Square
D. Reynolds Square
E. Warren Square
F. Washington Square
G. Telfair Square
H. Wright Square
I. Oglethorpe Square
J. Columbia Square
K. Greene Square

L. Orleans Square
M. Chippewa Square
N. Crawford Square
O. Pulaski Square
P. Madison Square
Q. LaFayette Square
R. Troup Square
S. Chatham Square
T. Monterrey Square
U. Calhoun Square
V. Whitefield Square

SAVANNAH SCENES

10 & 11 Savannah Skyline
52-55 Cotton Exchange
12 & 13 Oglethorpe Monument
14 Tomochichi Monument
15 Fort Wayne
16 & 17 Pirate's House
22 & 23 Haunted House
20 & 21 Colonial Cementery
34 & 35 Independent Presbyterian
Church
26-29 Christ Church
36 & 37 Wesley Monumental Church
76 & 77 Mickve Israel Synagogue
44 & 45 Isaiah Davenport House
46 & 47 Owens-Thomas House
56 & 57 Ramp at East Nroad Street
42 & 43 Scarbrough House
63 Greene-Meldrim House
78-83 Railroad Complex
66 & 67 Daisy's Birthplace
68 & 69 First Girl Scout Headquar-

ters
72 & 73 Comer-Hill House
70 & 71 Mercer-Williams House
92 & 93 Forsyth Fountain
84 & 85 Telfair Academy of Arts
& Sciences
86 & 87 Telfair Hospital
114 Confederate Monument
88 & 89 Old Chatham County Jail
90 & 91 East Charlton Lane
100 & 101 New Post Office
38 & 39 Volunteer Guard Armory
107 Barnard Hall
98 & 99 Gingerbread House
119 First Saturday
113 Sgt. Jasper Monument
108 & 109 Catherdral of St. John the
Baptist
30 & 31 John Wesley
18 & 19 Old East State Street
104 & 105 Johnny Mercer House

SPECIAL MEMORIALS AND PLACES OF INTEREST

Chatham Volunteer Monument
Factor's Walk
Celtic Cross
Confederate War Monument
Vietnam War Monument
Spanish-American War Monument
Marine Monument
Hidden Garden
Johnson Square
Byck House

Troupe Square
St. Patricks Day
Hidden Garden
Church of the Ascension
St. Johns Church
Monterrey Square
Around Forsyth Park
Champion/Fowlkes House
Shakespeare in the Park
From my sketchbook

6

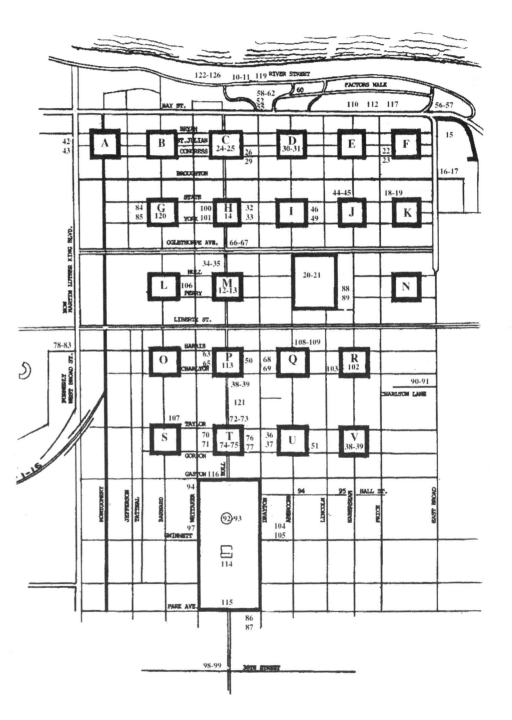

TABLE OF CONTENTS

7

The presentation of this seal to the Trustees gave them the authority to organize and manage the new colony of Georgia. Thus began the story of the City of Savannah.

When General Oglethorpe landed on the river bluffs, he founded Savannah in February of 1773.

Savannah remains as a leading city in the flow of commerce to and from all parts of the world.

COLONIA GEORGIA AUG.
(May The Georgia Colony Flourish)

NON SIBI SED ALIIS
(Not For Themselves, But For Others)

Introduction

I fell in love with her the first time I visited Savannah in the late 1960's. As an artist who spent several years in architectural drawing and renderings, I was drawn to Savannah like a magnet.

In the summer of 1979, I moved to Savannah to start an architectural antique business with my husband, Bill. This special business gave me a day-to-day involvement with Savannah history and architecture. Traveling to England to buy architectural treasures for our business, I experienced the exhilaration of actually seeing models of Savannah architecture. For it was the English tradesmen who built early Savannah and influenced the architecture. The English architect William Jay left a legacy in the designs of some of the noted buildings I painted and sketched in this book.

Unfortunately, as a business person, I could not find time to paint scenes of my adopted city as I longed to do.

With mixed emotions, I surveyed the loss of our business through a disastrous fire in 1990. The loss on one hand created sadness because of the loss of many historic architectural items from England's past as well as early American treasures which can never be replaced.

But, in retrospect I realized that the loss was my gain: I was at last free to paint this beautiful city.

These works vary in medium and technique. My years of architectural rendering reinforced my natural inclination toward preciseness and accuracy; however, to express the essence of a subject with a minimum of strokes is greatly to be admired. Most of these pictures are a combination between these two approaches.

I've moved trees and lamp posts and done away with a few objects here and there, but these works are essentially as Savannah is today.

I take a sketchbook with me wherever I go. From time to time I'll pick up my painting gear for painting on site. Painting comfort is in my studio where I can plan and concentrate on composition, unity and harmony. In this case I can use my sketches, notes and photographs for reference. It's also vital for me to evoke the memory of how I felt about the subject when I was moved to do a sketch or painting.

Louise Yancey Streed
1995

Trustee's Rules for the Colony of Georgia 1735

Labor, Clear and Fence the Land

Guard Against the Enemy

Set Self Up with Craft

Plant Mulberry Trees Upon 50 Acres and Other Such Crops

Hard Liquor, Such as Rum, Forbidden

No Slavery

No Unlicensed Trading with the Indians

No Lawyers in the Georgia Land.

9

What would Savannah be without the river? Wide and deep enough for international shipping it has been nurturing the city since its founding. This view from an isolated spot on Hutchinson Island gives me a better perspective of the old cotton warehouses and the daily rush of activity. I gaze from the tugboat mooring to the paddlewheel boats and further west to an electricity generating plant.

As I return by crossing over the bridge I see the tangle of happy tourists in the shops and restaurants. They look up to see the balconies on the sturdy weather beaten old warehouses and try to imagine how it was here in the 1850's when masted ships were loaded with bales of Georgia cotton.

General Oglethorpe more or less hand picked the original colonists who landed on the bluff of Savannah on February 12, 1733. Turbulent times were the order of the day which Oglethorpe took in stride. His tenure of 10 years established the rules and regulations which became basic to the survival and growth of the Georgia colony. He returned to England and continued to retain an interest in Georgia. He died at the age of 89 in 1786 and is buried in All Saints Church in Cranham. As an interesting anecdote, the church burned and was rebuilt and Oglethorpe's grave was lost. His grave remained lost for 138 years. Later found, it was marked and a memorial service is held there every year on February 12, Georgia Day.

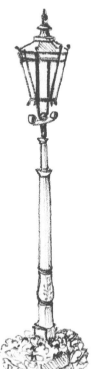

12

General James Oglethorpe

As we enter Chippewa Square, I see the presence of General James Oglethorpe in a greater than life bronze statue by Daniel Chester French. I could not help feeling a touch of awe as I painted this scene. Standing in a striking pose with his sword in hand, it seems that he does not need the protection of the four British lions which are mounted on the corners of the base. I feel in a sense that this great man still looks over the Savannah Scene. With the greatest satisfaction I paint this scene of strength and tranquility and think of those who helped found Savannah. I hope that in some small way I have recorded here a reminder of greatness, a loving tribute to the founders of Georgia.

13

Tomochichi

Tomochichi, Chief of the Yamacraws, lies in Wright Square which holds the oldest historic memory of Savannah. A friend of Oglethorpe and England, he was buried with full military honors in October of 1739 at the age of 97. It is said that the Gordon Monument in the center of the square supposedly displaced the original grave of Tomochichi and the large granite boulder in the corner of the square was placed there in retribution for the injustice done to Tomochichi's happy hunting ground.

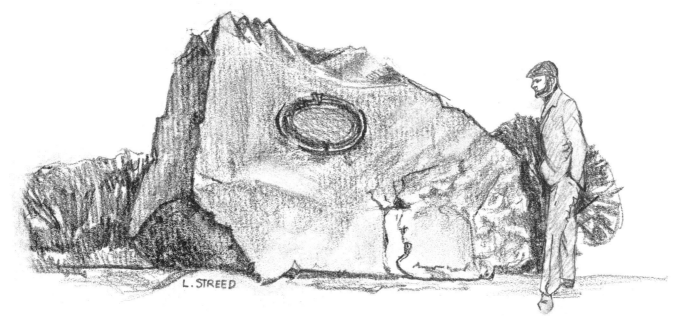

L. STREED

Historical Anecdote

"Tomochichi was ninety-one years old when he met Oglethorpe upon the colonists' landing on the bluff. He was tall, vigorous, dignified and manly. He was a true friend to the colonists, and aided them in making treaties with other tribes of indians. Let us not forget that while Oglethorpe deserves every praise as the leader of the colonists, yet this aged Indian Chief made the colony possible by his guarantee of safety and friendship to the colonists, and to him is due the lasting gratitude of their descendents."

14

Fort Wayne

These buttressed walls are those of Fort Savannah formed by a bluff on the original trustees Gardens. Built in 1762, it was renamed for General "Mad Anthony" Wayne who freed Savannah from the British in July of 1782. History records that "Mad Anthony" was apparently mad about the ladies. He squired many prominent ladies of the area during his several years in Savannah. He was awarded a plantation along the Savannah River as compensation for his contribution to the military success of the revolution. His controversial nature caused him all manner of problems, both financial and political...although he was elected to congress as a Georgia representative. His election was contested due to fraudulent voting procedures. He is remembered in Georgia by the city of Waynesboro. Wayne county was also named in his memory.

This quick sketch was executed on an extremely hot afternoon while sitting under a Pittisporum bush from across Bay Street.

Louise Y. Streed '94

15

The Pirates' House

The Herb House attached to the Pirates' House is reputed to be the oldest house in Georgia. This could well be since it was built in 1734 as the residence of the royal gardener for the Trustees Garden. It is said that it served also as a stopover for the infamous pirate Captain Flint and as the story goes, he died there.

The site on the flat above Old Fort Savannah now known as Fort Wayne overlooks the river from this high bluff. This area was the acreage set aside by the trustees as a nursery to develop fruit vines, mulberry trees, shrubs and crop seed for the colony.

My earlier visits to Savannah nearly always included a lunch at the Pirates' House. I always liked the view from East Broad Street as shown in the painting. I am intrigued by the architecture as well as the history. I painted the old brick and weather beaten wood with a touch of mistiness that I see in this interesting part of old Savannah; something here gives the feeling of a mysterious past that remains hidden.

© LOUISE Y. STREED 1994

Old East State Street

In this area of Savannah the colonists' activity was centered around the Trustees Garden, which is just around the corner of East State Street. The houses in this area that are original, such as those in the painting, are survivors of the fire of 1820 that virtually destroyed Savannah. The great oak in the painting was just a seedling when these houses were built in about 1818. The houses here are all occupied and kept in excellent repair, a living preservation.

I did this quick watercolor one afternoon from Greene Square. Just around the corner from my studio at that time in this quiet scene of the early 1800's.

LOUISE Y STREED
© 1994

19

Old Colonial Cemetery

This interesting cemetery is located fittingly at the corner of Oglethorpe Avenue and Abercorn Street, named for the earliest prominent figures in Savannah. The visitors in the painting are reading the plaque on the Graham vault. It was in this vault that Nathaniel Greene and his sons were interred for 114 years. In 1901 their remains were reinterred under the Greene Monument in Johnson Square. The Marquis de Lafayette of France laid the cornerstone for this monument upon his visit to Savannah in 1825. From 1750 through 1859 many of Georgia's illustrious were buried here. Among those were Button Gwinnett, signer of the Declaration of Independence, General Samuel Elbert, John Habersham, and Major John Berrien of the Continental Army. Also buried here is Edward Green Malbone, renowned painter of miniatures. Many unmarked vaults and graves instill an aura of mystery to this dedicated ground.

The complimentary contrast of the red brick against the early spring green and mossy oaks was appealing to me. This quiet and peaceful resting place gives a purpose for a painting of this unusual subject.

The Haunted House

This house was built in 1796 and escaped the disastrous fire of 1820. Could it be that the reported ghosts resented the fact that it was moved from East Bryan Street to its present location by Jim Williams in 1963?

Whatever ghost stories it may tell, I like it for its gambrel roof and its style that reminds me of New England. There are several homes in Savannah that have ghost stories to tell, several of which I have been told first hand. The intriguing story of this house adds to the interest I have in the architecture. Did I paint a ghost in the dormer or is that my imagination?

LOUISE Y. STREED © 1994

Nathaniel Greene Monument
In
Johnson Square

Johnson Square was named in honor of Governor Johnson of South Carolina as appreciation for his assistance to General Oglethorpe and the colonists in providing early requirements of the colony. Nathaniel Greene, a military genius of his time, was appointed by George Washington to serve as the leading general in the continental army in the southern most colonies. He remained in the Savannah area after the British were defeated and was awarded two plantations on the Savannah River that were confiscated from the Tory owners. The Mulberry Grove Plantation was the home of General Greene and on this plantation Eli Whitney invented the cotton gin. General Greene died on his plantation and was buried in the Graham Vault in the colonial cemetery. This monument was erected in 1825 with the Marquis de Lafayette laying the corner stone. General Greene and his son were reinterred under this monument in 1901.

This is my favorite square, not only because of its beauty, but also because its history is visible all around the square in the buildings of architectural significance. This square with its park-like atmosphere is a center of activity in the everyday life of Savannah. One may hear a musical group playing during the lunch hour while resting in the colorful shade of large oak trees. I made here a watercolor of the Greene Monument with the golden dome of City Hall in the background.

24

25

Christ Church
On
Johnson Square

Shortly after Oglethorpe landed at Savannah, the trustees granted to Christ Episcopal Church a lot on Johnson Square. On June 11, 1740 construction began. After many starts and stops due to a lack of finances, the church was completed and dedicated on the 7th of July in 1750. John Wesley came to Savannah in 1735 and administered to this parish of the Church of England. He is credited with writing a hymnal and establishing probably the first Sunday School in Christ Church.

The church was destroyed in a great fire of 1796. It was rebuilt and 100 years later was again destroyed by fire. Rebuilt and dedicated on May 23, 1898, it stands today on the same lot as did its original structure.

I sketched this view of the church from the center of the square. Even though it is almost hidden behind huge live oaks from where I sit, I can appreciate its classic features borrowed directly from ancient Greece.

LOUISE Y STREED © '94

Christ Church

The interior of Christ Church is a thing of beauty.
With its elegant stained glass over the alter, it makes
a most interesting composition of restrained color and
artistry.

I found myself deeply involved in bringing the
many details into a focused rendition of this beautiful
church. The church seems to stand as a sentinel overlooking this famous square. With the combined stately buildings and carefully attended beauty of the
square, it is easy to see why I am always tempted to
reach for a brush or pencil to record some aspect of
this scene.

LOUISE Y. STREEP © 1994

John Wesley

On February 5, 1736, Oglethorpe on his return from a visit to England, brought John Wesley and James Habersham. John Wesley came as a missionary; however, his duty as licensed was as a priest for the Church of England. While he was at first disappointed in not being involved as a missionary to the Indians, he administered to the church with enthusiasm. His enthusiasm and rigid adherence to the rules of the church eventually led to his being disliked by many of the colonists. He returned to England rather bitter and spent the remainder of his life in developing Methodism.

Even though his leaving was controversial, he planted the seed of religion in the area. His friend James Habersham, who accompanied Wesley to Savannah, became a pioneer in the commerce and trade in the growing Savannah and Georgia economy. Both John Wesley and James Habersham left an indelible mark on the continuing history of Savannah.

Savannah is a never ending opportunity for whetting the artist's appetite. I found myself in the beautifully shaded Reynolds Square where I could comfortably sketch not one but two objects of my interest. This sketch of the John Wesley Monument is fittingly the focal point with the Habersham ancestral home as the background. The Habersham House is now the Pink House Restaurant.

LOUISE Y. STREED © '94

Church of the Ascension

A small group of Salzburgers and Moravians who came to Savannah remained while the others founded the town of Ebenezer some 30 miles above Savannah. Most of the Moravians left and went to Pennsylvania.

Pastor Johann Martin Bolzius is credited with founding the church in Savannah after administering to the worshipers in Savannah from his church in Ebenezer. The recorded founding was April 14, 1741. The church originally purchased the old original courthouse which was built in 1736 and moved it to a lot which they purchased in 1771. This is the present location of the church. The Lutheran church grew and the present church is the result of several renovations, the last major change was in 1875.

The Lutheran church served not only its own congregation but when disastrous fires burned the Presbyterian church, the Lutheran church graciously provided its building for their services until their church could be restored. Other churches used the Church of the Ascension temporarily when their facilities were untenable for various reasons.

I drew the church while sitting in front of the old Cargill Office Supply. It soars above the trees and the county courthouse next door. The striking of the hour and chimes at the quarter hour made this a most pleasant task. The facade of the church is a symphony of movement in the changing shadows. The staccato decorations under the eaves are balanced by the rounded windows and massive volumes of the tower base and large engaged campaniles. The sun was coming from the east but still the shadows on the facade made an intriguing pattern. This is the most interesting facade in Savannah although the Cotton Exchange is a close second.

My sky treatment of vertical pencil strokes emphasizes the spirituality of this building.

LOUISE STREED © 1995

33

Independent Presbyterian Church

On January 16, 1756, a public lot was granted by the King of England for the Presbyterian Church. Construction was not begun till later and the church was dedicated in May of 1819, an event that was attended by President Monroe who was visiting Savannah at the time.

On June 24, 1884, future President Woodrow Wilson married the granddaughter of the Reverend Doctor Axon of the Presbyterian Church. The ceremony was performed in the manse.

The church was burned during the great fire of 1889 that destroyed the greater part of Savannah. Rebuilt and dedicated in 1891, its architecture and purpose combine to compliment the beauty of Savannah.

This painting shows a seldom noticed view of the Independent Presbyterian Church because the traffic flows counter clockwise around Chippewa Square. I framed the exquisite white spire between the Foley House and the church's educational building. The arched wall is an attractive base for the composition.

34

Wesley Monumental Church

Wesley Monumental Church has a history prior to January 19, 1868; however, this is the recorded date of its official organization. The cornerstone was laid on August 10, 1875. The congregation suffered many financial problems in building the present church. The congregation was led by the Reverend A. M. Wynn, who worked diligently with them to raise funds needed for construction. Their dedication efforts raised the required funds from far and wide, even from foreign countries. Reverend Wynn, the staunch leader, served from the early 1870s to 1877, after which he left for other calls. He returned in 1887 and saw the fulfillment of the congregational efforts as the church was finally consecrated on March 31, 1890 as a monument to John and Charles Wesley, early ministers in the colonies.

From Drayton Street looking east, the two steeples of this church rise above a row of stately palms, the best view of this church by far. The towers are not repeats of each other, but vary in height, size and design. Could they be the symbols of the two Wesley brothers?

It is very satisfying for me to draw this building swiftly with a soft 5B pencil. It gives me a strong, very black line which this monument calls for.

© LOUISE Y. STREED '94

37

Volunteer Guard Armory

The Savannah Volunteer Guard Armory was designed by architect William Gibbons Preston in 1892. This picturesque style by Preston is evident in the Cotton Exchange, old Chatham Court House and several residences in Savannah.

The guard, organized in 1805, distinguished itself in every military engagement since that time, including the Civil War. This armory replaced the original arsenal which was located on Whitaker Street. The cannon standing vertically on their cascabels at the entrance are themselves historic. Originally siege cannons on old Fort Wayne, they were removed to the arsenal on Whitaker Street when Fort Pulaski fell. They were buried in the basement of the arsenal where they were uncovered in 1884 and placed at the new armory when it was built.

The building is the first one acquired by the Savannah College of Art and Design in 1979. It continues to be an important part of the SCAD Campus. I enjoy the sight of it, with its exuberant display of curves and straights. The turrets, balconies and arches make it a very original interpretation of the Richardsonian Romanesque Style.

One day as I was admiring the building, the sight of two Savannah College of Art and Design students on the balcony forced me to drop my tote bag and begin an immediate quick sketch which I later executed with gouche on matte board.

Whitefield Square

Beautiful Whitefield Square (pronounced without the "e") diverts Habersham and east Wayne Streets. It was named after George Whitefield, an eloquent English preacher who was invited to the colonies by John Wesley. His concern for the many orphans in the area prompted him to work constantly in raising funds for the founding of Bethesda Home for Boys, which has been successfully providing care for boys to this day near the Isle of Hope.

My painting captures the Victorian style gazebo in the center of the square. The gazebo is often festooned for outdoor weddings and with Christmas decorations as a neighborhood project for the festivities.

In the background is the historically interesting First Congregational Church. Founded in 1868, it was the outgrowth of a missionary effort on behalf of the black population of the area. In 1867, Alfred E. Beach, Editor of the Scientific American Magazine, donated land and funds for the Beach Institute as a school for education of negroes who at that time had no such institutions.

The founders of the church for several years used the Beach Institute facilities for a meeting place. In 1878, a small wooden church was built. Replaced on the same lot, the new and present church was built in 1895.

41

Scarbrough House

L. STREED

This William Jay masterpiece called for another pencil sketch. It's in the classic regency style, which we see in several other houses in Savannah, but they all have an individuality which sets them apart.

Designed and built in 1819, this house has witnessed many important happenings in Savannah. Mr. Scarbrough was instrumental in building the steamship *Savannah*. From parties celebrating the sailing and return of the steamship *Savannah* to presidential parties for President James Monore, the Scarbrough House was a center of important social affairs.

As time and wealth passed the scene, the Scarbrough House became vacant, a school and again vacant. Saved by the Savannah Historic Foundation, it became a combination museum and headquarters for the foundation. Recently acquired by Ships of the Sea Museum, it may again become very active in Savannah history.

LOUISE Y STRAND © 1994

43

Isaiah Davenport House

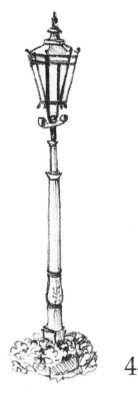

In 1819, Isaiah Davenport, a master builder, built his home on the corner of State and Habersham Streets. It stands as a tribute to the talent of the carpenter-architect of that era. Beautifully coordinated in style and proportion, it attracts the attention of all sightseers. It is open to the public today and is in part a museum and gift shop.

I stationed myself on the corner of President and Habersham. The sight of the Kehoe House, the present Davenport house and a corner of Columbia Square was more than I could resist. I began my drawing while thinking of how this historic Davenport House had been slated for demolition but rescued by people who were appalled at the thought of Savannah losing its heritage of fine old houses. Thus began the Historic Savannah Foundation. The Kehoe House was recently rescued from its vacant obscurity and is now an elegant inn. It is among the finest of Victoriana in the city, the former home of the president of Kehoe Iron Foundries where much of the city's iron railings, fences and gates originated.

LOUISE Y STREED © 1994

45

Owens-Thomas House

I chose to sketch with pencil the entrance of this wonderful regency house. The gracefully curved facade with an ovoid sculpted into the face of the building to form the entryway is further enhanced with curving double stairway and columned porch. This is my favorite aspect of the house. William Jay, the young English architect is credited with the design of the house as well as the Scarbrough House and Telfair House, all of which reflect his genius for fine detail.

The following pages show other parts of the house which holds many reminders of the history of Savannah. My interest in architectural details makes the Owens-Thomas house a continuous reminder to me of the artistic differences in architectural styles which are benchmarks of history.

The Owens-Thomas house is used in almost all architectural text books as the perfect example of Regency.

LOUISE Y STREED
© '94

47

Owens-Thomas House

To capture the elegance of the Owens-Thomas House, I painted the persimmon painted walls of the upstairs library with its coordinated color scheme and rugs. This beautiful library brings to me thoughts of the many occasions that brought delight to those who were guests here in the 19th century.

Among the distinguished guests was the Marquis de Lafayette, who, upon his visit to Savannah in March of 1825, spoke to a crowd from the balcony.

His visit as a guest was by proclamation of both houses of the legislature.

This house is a must when visiting Savannah and is open to the public.

The Lafayette Balcony

48

LOUISE Y STREED © 1994

The Eliza Jewett House

On Madison Square stands this interesting house constructed by the lady builder Eliza Jewett in 1842. It is considered an outstanding example of Greek Revival Style. Charles Clusky, an excellent Irish architect who built many famous homes in Savannah, is thought to be the architect of this house. In 1957 it was purchased from famed actor and Savannahian Charles Coburn who inherited it from his sister. It was one of the first projects in the planned restoration of historic buildings in Savannah.

It is presently owned by Edwin and Esther Shaver as their residence. Their prominent bookstore built in the former garden of this handsome residence is in the heart of the historic district.

This pencil sketch shows the classic features of the home which reflects the elegance of the past that is preserved in Savannah today.

50

(COURTESY OF MR. & MRS. EDWIN SHAVER)

The Byck House

This house, situated on Calhoun Square across the square from Wesley Monumental Church and across the street from old Massey School, is referred to as the Byck House because it was in the Byck family for many years.

I sketched it with its two story stacked porches which were the popular trend in the mid 1800s. Built in 1868 for Benjamin J. Wilson, it has the charm for which Savannah is known. My pencil drawing here interprets my feeling of respect for the architects and builders of early Savannah.

(COURTESY OF MRS. ELLEN BYCK)

51

Cotton Exchange Solomon's Lodge Number One

Here I drew the Savannah Cotton Exchange with its intricate facade. It was built in 1886 during the heyday of King Cotton. Cotton bales from all over the south arrived in Savannah and were auctioned to brokers at the exchange. This established international prices for cotton. The factors in offices on Factors Walk facilitated warehousing and shipping.

Solomon's Masonic Lodge now utilizes the building. The lodge was founded in 1734 in Sunbury, GA., which at that time was a thriving city. The lodge was officially chartered in England with General Oglethorpe as founder and first Master.

Moved later to Savannah, its name was changed from "Lodge at Savannah in Ye Province of Georgia" to Solomon's Lodge Number One. It is reported to be the oldest continuous Masonic Lodge in the United States. It was moved in 1975 to the Old Cotton Exchange.

Preston indulged his love of Romanesque here again with its red brick terra cotta and distinctive arching. It is build on iron columns with a street passing underneath.

LOUISE Y. STREED © 1994

The Cotton Exchange

On these two pages I test two mediums, pencil and watercolor. I first must recognize the works of Eli Whitney, who released the energy of the rural South when he invented the cotton gin on General Nathaniel Greene's Mulberry Grove Plantation at the suggestion of Mrs. Greene. I depict here in pencil the cotton boll at full burst. Also this gives me the idea to draw the original cotton gin. This device was instrumental in the start of the industrial revolution by allowing one person to clean 100 pounds of cotton per day, instead of less than one pound per day as done by hand. I feel the excitement that the cotton gin caused. In the watercolor on the next page, I show the unusual stained glass window on the north side of the Cotton Exchange.

Cotton Exchange

L. STREED © 1994

This stained glass was a target on my list to paint. Its beautiful colors, with the word "Cotton" entwined in the design is a delight to behold. This section of the window is about 10 feet wide by 5 feet. I was privileged to be given the approval for the painting by the Lodge historian Mr. Robert Porter. Besides the interest in the stained glass, I do a quickie sketch of the large mahogany chair in which General George Washington was seated during his visit to the Lodge in 1791 when the Lodge was located in a different part of Savannah.

East Broad Street Ramp

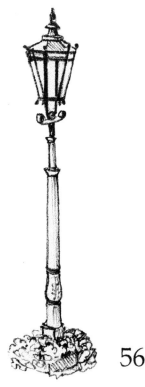

The easternmost ramp from Bay Street to the river has a natural and man-made texture as well as a geometric artistry. This is a structure that combines the non-uniform parts into a uniformly contoured facade of singular beauty. Where did these stones come from, what stories of labor and travel could they tell if they could speak? Above the ramp, I paint the cast iron post and lamp of the harbor light that was erected as a beacon for ships to avoid sunken ships from the Revolutionary war.

Sailing ships from around the world delivered their goods to Savannah. When only partly laden, or entering the port empty to carry cargo away, the hulls had to have ballast to remain stable at sea. Sailing ships loaded stone from their country or port of sailing since this type of ballast could be hand loaded as required to balance the forces of wind and sea. Early in the history of Savannah, little was imported and much stone accumulated as ships unloaded ballast and took on naval stores and other items they purchased in Savannah. They left the ballast stones which were used for buildings and later, until the middle 1800s, they were used as retaining walls, ramps and streets along the river.

LOUISE Y STREED

Factors Walk

In this and following pen and sepia wash pictures, I wanted to capture the contrasting angularity of the stone, walkways and structural elements of this area of riverfront buildings.

The original colonists had great difficulty scaling the forty foot bluff above the river. It was not long before they had carved steps reinforced with stone up the bluff and erected a crane to move supplies from the ships to the top of the bluff.

The present warehouses were built between the river and the bluff and are reached by walkways from Bay Street, which we call Factors Walk. They lead to the offices of the cotton "Factors" or brokers who handled the sale of imports and exports.

This is the Lincoln street ramp which is an exit from Bay Street. The angles formed by the intersection of wall and the walkways is a contrast in shape and tone of shadow. I find it a most interesting composition.

L. STREED '94

Under Factors Walk

I enjoyed doing this pen and sepia wash sketch of a unique view of the warehouse shipping and receiving side. The stone paved area where the autos are parked was the alley that was used by horse and wagon hucksters who picked up or delivered goods to the warehouses.

One can see the access ramps from Bay Street over the alleys and the generally fancy ironwork used as safety railings on the walk ways. These views are more interesting if you picture the bustle of men and horses vying for a place to wait for their turn to go to the warehouse door for loading and unloading.

L. STREED © 1994

I find the shadowy look under the Factors Walk a delightful exercise in mixing several methods of construction. I studied with interest the framing under the walkways and the delicate looking iron railing on the retaining walls and access stairway to Bay Street. This is the Drayton Street section leaving the Cotton Exchange.

61

This is the most interesting view of the Drayton Street portion that is directly under the Cotton Exchange. I try to picture the architect faced with designing the building on extended columns for free access to the river from the back of the warehouse.

L. STREED © 1994

Green-Meldrim House

The Green-Meldrim House is an elegant gothic Revival house designed by John S. Norris, well known architect who designed many homes in Savannah. The delicate ironwork and oriel windows enhance the strong design of this house. To give a partial view with an interesting framing, I sketched the off-street entrance through one of the arcades of the breezeway from the St. John Episcopal Church. I used pen and ink with a sepia wash to accentuate the iron fretwork.

St. John's Episcopal Church
&
Green-Meldrim House

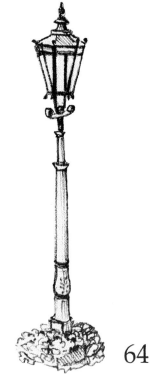

The St. John's Episcopal Church in this sketch is drawn from Pulaski Square. I like this composition framed in the moss from the oaks in the square and taking in a rear view of the Green-Meldrim house now owned by St. John's Church.

The church was chartered on November 26, 1846 and the cornerstone was laid March 23, 1852 indicating that the Charles Green home was being built about the same time, being finished in 1853.

St. John's was renovated in the late 1800s and the exceptional stained glass in the church was made in England and installed in 1880.

I enjoyed doing this scene while wondering at the apprehension of those in Savannah when Charles Green met with General William T. Sherman of the Union Army to surrender the city to prevent its destruction and the loss of his cotton. He saved the city but Sherman confiscated his cotton.

It is open to the public and is a featured stop for visitors to Savannah.

L. STREED © '94

65

Juliette Gordon Low Birthplace

As far back as I care to admit, Juliette Gordon Low was my idol. Daisy, as she was known to her close friends, was a remarkable person. I wanted to paint her birthplace with its lovely back porch overlooking the parterre garden. Built for James Moore Wayne in 1821, it was later purchased by the Gordons and Juliette was born there on October 31, 1860.

Juliette Gordon Low founded the Girl Scouts in 1912 and served the group until her death in 1927.

When I was a Girl scout, I did not have the opportunity to visit Savannah so I was delighted at the chance to put my feelings into this painting. The fact isn't documented but I feel that it was designed by William Jay. It has his regency style except for the graceful interior staircase, which we see in neither of Owens-Thomas House of Scarbrough house, both of which are documented as William Jay accomplishments.

LOUISE Y. STREED © 1995

First Girl Scout Headquarters

Some of my best times were with the Girl Scouts as a scout and later a scout leader. And here I am where it all started. Sitting between two parked autos on Charlton Street, I sketched "Daisy's" carriage house wondering if it was the same peach colored stucco in the days when she was organizing the scouts.

In this instance, I opted for a pencil sketch to show the informality of this building.

As I sketch I also muse about this remarkable woman, her varied talents and contributions and why there is no statue of her in this city where her works are remembered daily by the people who visit the mecca of Girl Scouting.

L. STREED © 1994

69

Mercer-Williams House

L. STREED

Designed by the noted architect John S. Norris and built for Confederate General Hugh Mercer in 1860 in the Italianate style. General Mercer, the grandfather of noted songwriter Johnny Mercer, did not reside in this magnificent house, selling it to others before it was completed.

Eventually purchased and refurbished by Jim Williams, a leader in the Savannah restoration period. Jim Williams, a wealthy antique dealer used this elegant house as a residence and the showroom for his antiques which he collected both here and abroad.

A tragic violent death of an associate occurred in the study of this house in 1981. Jim Williams was accused of murder, but was acquitted after four trials. Shortly thereafter, Jim Williams died suddenly in this house.

LOUISE V STREED 1994

71

The Comer House

The Hugh M. Comer House stands on Taylor Street facing Monterrey Square.

Former Confederate president Jefferson Davis, a friend of Hugh Comer, while visiting Savannah with his daughter Winnie, stayed in this house. The visit was during the centennial celebration of the Chatham Artillery with elaborate ceremonies held in famous Johnson Square.

Hugh M. Comer, a textile industrialist, established a major manufacturing complex in Alabama after the Civil War which is still a major factor in the economy of Alabama.

The Hill family, present owners, have preserved the house in its original condition and have obtained many of the original furnishings which are now in this house.

I sat in the square to sketch this interesting house which is typical Savannah with its stacked porches facing east to escape the hot sun in the afternoon.

L. STREED © 1994

73

Monterrey Square
&
Pulaski Monument

Monterrey Square is centered around many points of interest so I find myself there often when time is available. I have painted several of the surrounding historic buildings on my visits to this square.

The impressive monument in the square was placed there in memory of Count Casimir Pulaski, Polish count who was sent to Charleston, South Carolina and later to Savannah by General George Washington to aid in the battle for the recapture of of the city from the British. In this battle, many patriots were killed in the repulse of their efforts at the Spring Hill Redoubt. Count Pulaski was wounded severely and was removed to a French naval vessel where he was to be carried to Charleston for treatment. He died aboard ship and was buried at sea. This monument's cornerstone was laid by the Marquis de Lafayette on his visit to savannah in 1825 as he was also a friend of Count Pulaski.

The Pulaski Monument in Monterey Square. Savannah, Georgia

Mickve Israel
Synagogue

Seated on a bench in Monterrey Square, I painted the focal point of the Jewish synagogue. My painting here is motivated by my delight in the gothic style building topped with a Moorish steeple. It presents quite a beautiful effect against the sky.

This outstanding architectural triumph has an important place in history. It is reported that it is either the first or second oldest Jewish synagogue in the nation. It is also the only Gothic style synagogue in the country. On July 11, 1733, led by Samuel Nunez, forty Jews arrived in Savannah by chartered ship bringing the religious Covenants and the Ark to found the first Jewish congregation.

They worshiped without a synagogue until 1820 when the first synagogue was built on Liberty Street. This building facing Monterrey Square was consecrated on April 11, 1878.

Central Railroad & Canal Company

Chartered on December 20, 1833, the Central Railroad and Canal Company was founded. William W. Gordon, grandfather of Juliette Gordon Low, was its first president who guided its rapid growth. By 1843 a railroad trackage to Macon, Georgia was completed and at that time was the longest railroad in the world built by one company.

From 1850 to 1856 William Wadley designed the roundhouse complex on West Broad Street and Louisville Road. This complex was acclaimed as the most complete and elegant facility in the country.

As the diesel replaced the steam engine and highway transport became a competitor, the need for the complex gradually declined and became redundant, ceasing activity in the late 1970s. Registered as an important historical site, it is recognized as one of the best preserved railroad complexes of its era in the United States.

With my profound interest in history, particularly when it involves architecture, I prepared the following vignettes of a part of history in the field of transportation. The old buildings still stand though some are roofless, their shadows seem to protect the re-mains of a dynamic era of Savannah. The unique tower for the steam boiler chimney intrigues me with its intricate brickwork. The arch was a common motif in the mid 19th century and here it is used to perfection. Attention to decorative detail in industrial buildings was as much an imperative as for the public buildings and houses.

old Roundhouse Savannah

78

Ruins at Roundhouse Complex - Savannah

Louise Yancey

Base of Roundhouse Complex Savannah   Louise Yancey

Louise Yancey

Roundhouse Complex

Nancy Hanks
The End Of A Railroad Era

The Nancy Hanks was a passenger train service from Savannah to Atlanta named after a famous trotting horse. It began in 1892, discontinued in 1893 due to trackage problems and revived in 1947 with the use of diesel locomotives. It made its final run on April 30, 1971 due to sagging revenues and auto and air travel. This was the end of the railroad passenger service era by private companies.

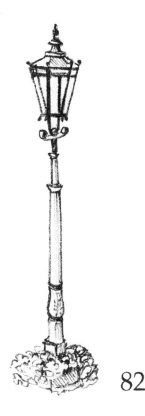

Telfair Academy Of Arts And Sciences

The Telfair Academy of Arts and Sciences was dedicated on May 3, 1886, making it the first museum of art in Georgia. Bequeathed to Savannah by the Telfair family, along with more than a million dollars in cash and investments for development of the academy. I show here a pen drawing of this excellent mark in architecture as executed by William Jay in the early 1800s. This was the mansion of the Telfair family who were active in all phases of government from the time of the Revolutionary War. Edward Telfair was Governor of Georgia and the building was given to the city by Miss Mary Telfair. The word "Admirable" describes the contribution to Savannah and Georgia by this illustrious family.

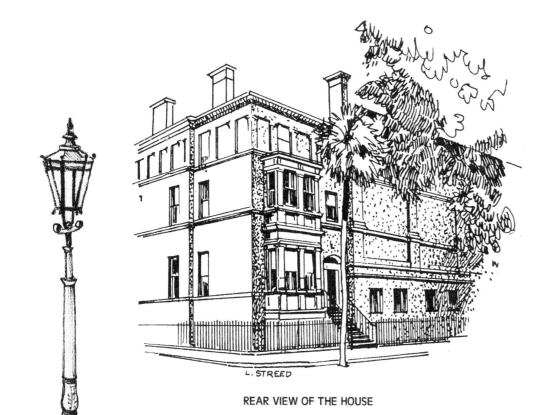

L. STREED

REAR VIEW OF THE HOUSE

84

TELFAIR
ACADEMY OF ARTS & SCIENCES

LOUISE YANCEY

85

Telfair Hospital For Women

The Telfair Hospital for Women, located on the corner of Park Avenue and Drayton Streets, was designed in 1884. Fay & Eichberg Architects designed the building which was built at a cost of $31,000. The hospital is thought to be the first hospital for women in the country and was a gift of Miss Mary Telfair, spinster member of the the Telfair family. This hospital served continuously for 96 years until 1960 when it was acquired by Candler Hospital. It was closed in 1980 when Candler moved into consolidated facilities on DeRenne Avenue. The building has been maintained in its exterior facade although it is now an apartment complex.

TELFAIR

TELFAIR HOSPITAL

LOUISE Y. STREED © 1994

87

Old Chatham County Jail

This painting captures a view I saw every day when driving home from the studio. Now only bare roofless walls are where the cells once were, but the exciting victorian tower survives. The spires of the cathedral in the distance repeat the vertical. This is a quick watercolor vignette done on hot pressed paper.

The jail was designed in 1886 by the McDonald Brothers Architectural Firm from Louisville, Kentucky, who won a competition for the commission which stated that the cost was not to exceed $60,000. It was constructed for $47,000. How time change. A brief description of the jail was noted as follows: "A stone structure with quoined corners and simple fenestration. The most striking feature is the domed watchtower. The circular tower rises from the main block of the building, the transition is made by four rectangular buttresses which are pierced by bullseye windows. Iron balconies rest on top of each buttress. Four arched doorways open onto the balconies. The dome is almost Byzantine in configuration. The design is among the firm's finest." This description is ample reason for me to go to brush and palette.

LOUISE Y. STREED © 1993

89

East Charlton Lane

On the eastern side of Savannah there remains a picture of the past in carpenter vernacular type cottages. Many of these are among the oldest buildings in Savannah.

Here on East Charlton Lane I particularly like the contrast of the sandy street with the bright colors of the slanting porches. The angularity of roofs and shed type additions, as well as natural weathering of some of the exterior wood, adds character to the neighborhood.

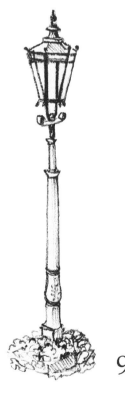

Forsyth Fountain

This magnificent cast iron fountain was perhaps inspired by the fountain on the Place de la Concorde Esplanades in Paris.

It was dedicated in 1858 in the Forsyth Park to the memory of John Forsyth, a former governor of Georgia who also became one of the two Georgians who became Secretaries of State for the United states. (The other Secretary of State from Georgia was Dean Rusk.)

I often walk in Forsyth Park and never tire of gazing at the cascading fountain. In making this painting, I made sure that the background trees were very dark to "snap" out the form of the fountain. To give the effect of water spray, I used a razor blade on the completely dry background. This required heavy 300# cold pressed textured paper.

92

© LOUISE Y STREED 1993

Around Forsyth Park

On the four streets bordering Forsyth Park— Gaston Street, Whitaker Street, Drayton Street and Park Avenue— a picture of various architectural styles record the heyday of the City of Savannah.

I could spend months painting the varied styles of Romanesque, Greek Revival, Victorian and other periods that are reflected in this area. I quickly paint here an interesting detail of a house on Whitaker street on the west side of the park.

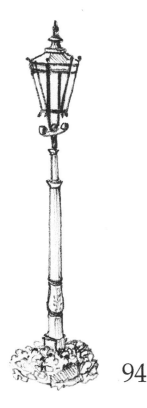

Sycamore In Savannah

I painted this watercolor of a sycamore tree in the foreground of some elegant houses in the Victorian historic district of Savannah. I find the varied shades of the tree caused by the shedding of bark an interesting composition. With the soft colors of the sycamore, I painted a misty view through which I see the houses in the background.

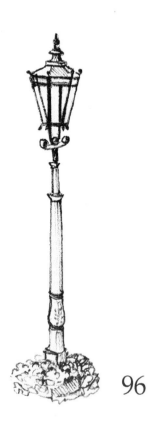

On Abercorn Street

Savannah gives the artist a chance to practice the painting of architecture that spans two hundred years of history. I particularly like to picture the interesting elements of construction such as in this painting of a Victorian house on Abercorn Street whose architect was influenced by the Queen Anne Style.

I'm attempting to see Savannah through the eyes of the architect of that time.

97

The Gingerbread House

Here I execute two different representations of the same subject because of the unique design of this house. These watercolors describe the Gingerbread house on the corner of Bull and 36th Streets. In the Steamboat Gothic Style, I find two feelings: one of admiration for the workmanship required to construct this work and on the next page my reaction to the extravagant detail.

LOUISE YANCEY

The Gingerbread House intrigues the artists and photo buffs due to its prominent location among mixed architectural styles and its overdose of intricate fretwork. I painted this one somewhat out of focus because so much exuberance had a dizzying effect.

99

Post Office

This building, which stands on the west side of Wright Square, was built in two parts. The left front side being added as an image of the right side except that faux stone was apparently used in the most recent addition. Interestingly, we recovered the stained glass that was in the original building which this new one replaced in 1880. We restored several of the arched stained glass but unfortunately, the fire that destroyed our business also consumed the remainder of these treasures.

Around the corner of the York Street side is a face carved into the facade, a feature seldom seen and pointed out to me by Dr. John Duncan who assisted me in defining historical facts. We think it represents Uncle Sam.

This square, named for one of the first leaders in Savannah, boasts a monument to William W. Gordon, founder of the central of Georgia Railroad, and in one corner the granite stone memorial of Chief Tomochichi. Also facing the square on the east is the Lutheran Church of the Ascension, the old County courthouse built in 1887 and the ornate Wachovia Bank Building. I want to put them all on paper.

L.STREED

LOUISE Y STREED © '94

Troup Square

Troup Square was named after George M. Troup, one of the more powerful governors of early Georgia. First elected by the state legislators in 1823, he was the first governor elected by the people in a direct voter election in 1825. In 1827 he was the first "States Rights" governor when he defied president Adams and won his terms on acquisition of Creek Indian lands.

In the background across the square we see the "Jingle Bells Church" so named because James G. Pierpont, a member of this church, wrote the renowned tune "Jingle Bells." He was musical director of the Unitarian Church in the 1850s which, at that time, was on Oglethorpe Square. His brother, John Pierpont, was pastor of this church. James Pierpont served in the Confederate Army and was married to the daughter of Mayor Purse of Savannah.

In this pencil drawing I use as a foreground focal point the unique cast iron ornamental water bowl bollard with two water bowls for the convenience of small pets when visiting the park. This canine fountain was a gift to the city of Savannah from Mayor Herman Myers in 1869.

LOUISE Y. STREED

103

Johnny Mercer House

Savannah's own Johnny Mercer was one of the most prolific song writers of his time. His songs are memorable in both stage plays and in musical arrangements around the world. The list of songs he wrote is too long to enumerate, but below are some of my favorite Johnny Mercer songs:

I'm An Old Cowhand	Moon River
Bob White	Fools Rush In
You Must Have Been A Beautiful	Blues In The Night
Baby	Dearly Beloved
And The Angels Sing	That Old Black Magic
Day In, Day Out	Autumn Leaves

This pencil drawing shows Johnny's boyhood home at the corner of Gwinnett and Lincoln Streets. I sketched the scene of the ladies with their tea on the front porch as I imagine was a typical scene of the times when Johnny was growing up in Savannah.

LOUISE Y STREED © 1994

Champion/Fowlkes House

The Champion/Fowlkes House was designed by John B. Clusky, Irish architect who lived on the McAlpin plantation known as *The Hermitage*.

On this plantation he designed and made his ironworks to enhance the many famous homes he created for Savannah.

The Champion House was purchased for her residence by Aleta Fowlkes, one of the most enthusiastic leaders of the restoration movement in Savannah. She continued her interest in preservation until her death.

I drew this sketch as I reminisced about this polite, vibrant lady whom I met and visited in this wonderful house. To her perseverance Savannah owes a great debt of gratitude.

LOUISE Y STREED © 1995

106

Barnard Hall

Located on the corner of Taylor and Barnard Streets on Chatham Square, this Mediterranean Revival styled building was designed by Gottfried L. Norman in 1906.

It served as the Barnard Street Elementary School until the late 1980s. It was acquired by the Savannah College of Art and Design as an art department school. This reuse of the older building in Savannah aids greatly in the preservation of not only their structure but the purpose as well. I admired the architecture which is a departure from the architecture generally associated with old Savannah.

L. STREED © '94

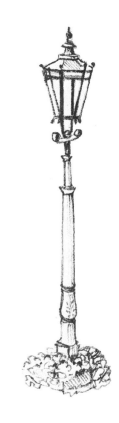

107

Cathedral Of
St. John The Baptist

Upon entering this beautiful church, I stand in awe as I absorb the magnificence of the nave. The groined vaulting, the stained glass reaching for the sky, the great rose window and the frescoes on the walls all rival the cathedrals of Europe which I visited. This is French Gothic construction at its best and brings together the feeling of the spiritual and man in harmony.

Although the Parish of St. John the Baptist was established in the late eighteenth century, the present cathedral was not built until construction started in 1874, being completed in 1896. Only two years after completion, it was nearly destroyed by fire, leaving only a shell but sparing the rose window and the spires. It was rebuilt and rededicated in 1900.

For this viewpoint I sat on the chancel steps and looked toward the narthex.

108

LOUISE Y STREED © '94

109

Celtic Cross

The Celtic Cross is classically Irish and brings to me a vision of Irish monks during the middle ages illuminating their manuscripts with the same entwined ribbons and ropes that I'm attempting to draw now. I had the same vision when in Ireland and saw abbey ruins which had been destroyed by Oliver Cromwell in the 16th century.

This cross in Emmett Park was dedicated in December of 1983. It was commissioned by the Savannah Irish Monument Committee and was acquired through the efforts of Milton Little. It was carved in Boyle County, Roscommon, Ireland of Irish limestone, most likely quarried in County Kilkenny, Ireland. Mr. Little assisted in the final design and arranged for production and shipment from Ireland.

L.Y. STREED

St. Patricks' Day

I love a parade. I also like the many shades of green with the complimentary and contrasting colors in harmony. These quick watercolor paintings capture the unfettered antics of young and old alike in Savannah's St. Patricks' Day Parade reputed to be one of the largest Irish celebrations in America. Of course, why not? Everyone can be Irish for at least one day.

111

Chatham Artillery Monument

Located in Emmett Park is the memorial to the Chatham Artillery, dedicated on May 4, 1986 to the memory of those who served in every war in which our country was involved, beginning with the Revolutionary War.

INSCRIPTION

Soldiers in War
Patriots in Peace

112

Sgt. Jasper Monument

The Jasper Monument in Madison Square memorializes one of the best known heroes in the Battle for Savannah in 1779.

Sargent Jasper, also a hero in fighting the battle of Fort Moultrie, South Carolina, was killed while retrieving the flag of his regiment at the retreat from the redoubt. This redoubt, know as the Springfield Redoubt, was located near the visitors center along Louisville Road.

Jasper Spring, west of Savannah, is named in his honor as is Jasper County, South Carolina.

113

Confederate Monument

L. STRELT © 1994

Shortly after the end of the Civil War, the Ladies Memorial Association raised some $21,000 for a monument to the Confederate soldier. Not wanting to use a Northern stone, they commissioned Robert Reid of Montreal Canada to sculpt it from Canadian stone. It was shipped by sea rather than have it pass through the Northern states, although it cost $1,000 in customs duty.

Dedicated on May 12, 1875, it was a heartfelt disappointment to the ladies because its two statues did not give them the sensitive feeling they expected. The carved statue of "Silence" was atop the monument and the second statue, "Judgment", placed below in the columned section. G. Wimberly DeRenne, seeing the distress it caused to the ladies, offered to replace and pay for the statues with a bronze replica of a Confederate soldier. David Richards, a Welsh sculpture, then cast the statue as it is seen today.

The removed statues were then used as further memorials to the Confederate soldier. "Silence" now stands in the Confederate soldiers section of Laurel Grove Cemetery where some 650 Confederates rest. "Judgment" is in Thomasville, Georgia to mark the resting place of their Confederate dead.

Two statues of prominent military men from Savannah are placed around this Forsyth Park Monument. On the south side is the bust of Colonel Francis S. Bartow who, along with several other Savannahians, fell at the first Battle of Manasses. On the north side is the bust of Major General Lafayette McLaws who survived.

114

Spanish American War Monument

Located on the south side of Forsyth Park is the Spanish American War Monument. This heroic sized bronze statue of a soldier in the Spanish American War salutes those who served their country from 1898 to 1902.

Bronze plaques were later added as special tributes to William Grayson and Stephen N. Harris who served in the war and afterwards in service to the veterans of the war.

L. STREED ©1994

115

Marine Corps Memorial

This monument to the United States Marine Corps, which generally is the vanguard of military action, is located on the Gaston Street side of Forsyth Park. The marble memorial pays tribute to the Marines who fought and those who died in World War II, the Korean War and the Vietnam War.

It was erected by the Savannah detachment of the Marine Corps League and dedicated in 1947. An additional bronze plaque was added in honor of the Vietnam War casualties. This plaque was dedicated on November 11, Veterans Day in 1978.

L STREED

116

As I sketched this beautiful memorial in Emmett Park, I could feel the same mixed emotions that are always associated with this war. This stone memorial, topped by the bronze helmet, rifle and boots of a fallen soldier, is surrounded by a water-filled pool that signifies the isolation of the Vietnam War. The circular brick walkway has the engraved names of donors who made this monument possible. This memorial

Vietnam Memorial

was dedicated in 1990 as a tribute from the people of Savannah memorializing those who served and the more than 100 men from the area who made the supreme sacrifice.

L. STREED

117

Savannah Symphony Orchestra On River Street

There is nothing like the Savannah Symphony performing on River Street, a special night that I will someday paint in watercolor. People crowd the river front on symphony night with their own dinner and wine arranged wherever space permits. Thousands attend these free concerts of one of the leading symphony orchestras in the State of Georgia. Sometimes the finale is followed by a profusion of colorful fireworks. On this night, I decided to sketch.

First Saturday
On River Street

I made this quick watercolor of the dynamic scene which is a regular happening on River Street in Savannah on the first Saturday of each month. Arts and crafts along with food concessions in assorted tents and stalls liven the plaza which I captured as the moving visitors constantly changed the view and the colors

Shakespeare In The Park

I took my sketch book to Telfair Square to quickly sketch the City Lights Theater group perform Romeo and Juliet. We bring our own chairs, picnic blankets and refreshments to enjoy an evening in a Savannah square. The performance is free to the public and enjoyed by all.

120

Before leaving the center of the city, I must paint a hidden garden for which Savannah is noted. Several years ago, I drew the plans for hidden gardens as published in a book on the subject. This experience moved me to do a watercolor of a parterre garden. I painted this garden as it would look on a spring morning with the azaleas and peach trees blooming.

Hidden Gardens

Browsing the streets of historic Savannah, I quite often see an iron gate through which one is given a glimpse of a walled garden...a private place in the midst of a busy city.

From My Sketchbook

I take my sketch book everywhere. I love the dynamic waterfront with its ever changing scenes of ships and people. Here I make a montage of things that interest me at the spur of the moment as I visit the riverfront.

122

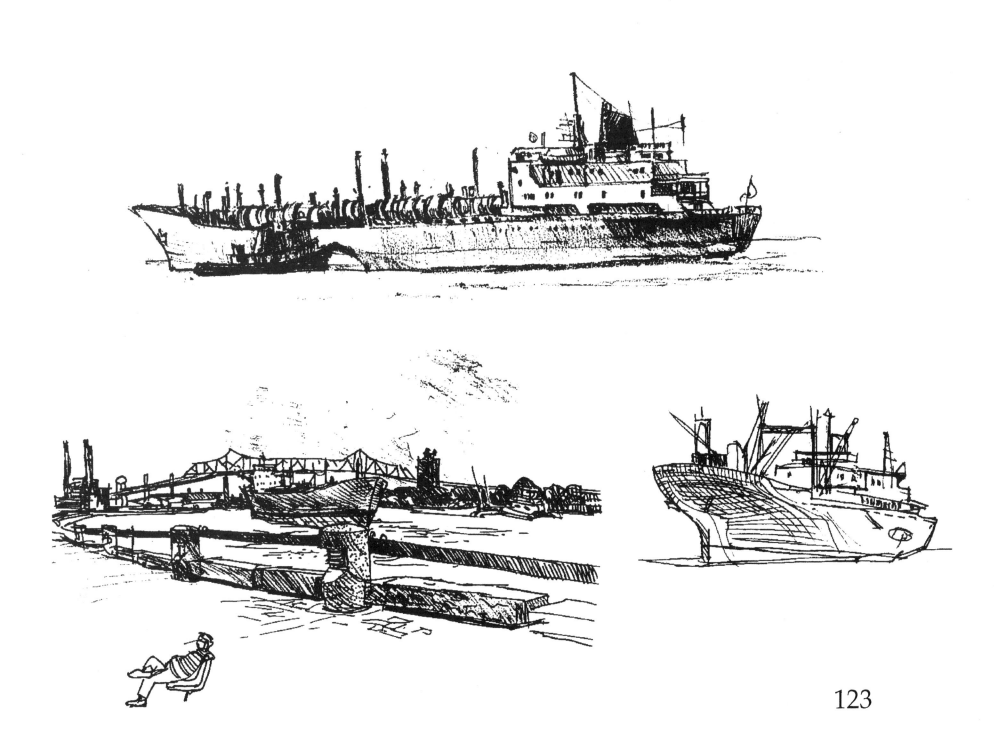

From My Sketchbook

These random sketches are made quickly to catch an object or person that is a fleeting subject or perhaps a permanent part of Savannah as I see it.

History In The Making

This and the following page reflect my interest in the new as well as the old. The building of the new suspension bridge over the Savannah River was a marvel in construction which had my attention for the duration of the project. The unique traveling form that inched its way across the river from each side was a picture I wanted to record as Savannah moved ahead into the new era that will in years to come be a subject of the history of this time.

I felt that this would be a fitting close to this book through my sketch of the new bridge and the old Talmadge Bridge which it replaces shown in the background. I feel the presence of the past with the demolition of the old bridge and the upbeat feeling of the exciting future that the new bridge will oversee until such time that it will itself be history.

126

Bibliography And Credits

The Savannah, (Thomas L. Stokes, 1951)
Stories of Georgia, (Joel Chandler Harris, 1896)
Georgia, A Pageant of Tears, (Mary Savage Anderson, 1933)
This is Your Georgia, (Bernice McCullar, 1966)
Savannah Morning News
Savannah Revisited, (Beehive Press, 1973)
Georgia Historical Society
Georgia History, (Lawton B. Evans, 1913)
America And Its People, (James Kirby Martin, Landy Roberts, Steven Mintz, Linda O. McMurray, James H. Jones, 1989)
New Viewpoints in Georgia History, (Albert N. Saye)

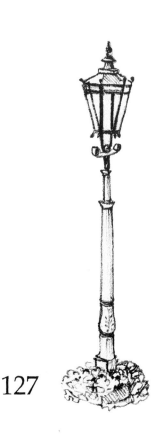

Thank you for visiting us here in Savannah